The Fortune Bird

Diana Bell Brooks

The Fortune Bird

Acknowledgements

Thanks to the following organisations for their support during the
writing of the poems in this book:

NSW Litlink and NSW Parks and Wildlife; Poetry Australia and
the Wollongong Workshops; Varuna, the Writers House; Australian
Poetry; Central West Writers Centre and Central West Libraries;
Cafe Latte, Orange.

Some of these poems have appeared online, in anthologies,
in the Katoomba Kiosk Poets self-published chapbook *Cloudland*,
and in Poems on the Menu in Cafe Latte
(as part of the AP Café Poets program).

I would also like to thank the members of writers groups in
Katoomba, and Vanessa Kirkpatrick in particular, for their many
helpful suggestions.

Special thanks are due to Deb Westbury for her presence
and her patience as the book developed.

Thanks also to Peter Bishop at Varuna, Sr Maureen Sheimer, Anne
Burke, Jan Richards and Jasmine Vidler at Central West Writers
Centre and Aaron Wright of Cafe Latte, and Hennie Moore, for their
encouragement, and to my family and friends for their ongoing support.

For Stephen, Daphne, Erin and William

The Fortune Bird
ISBN 978 1 74027 821 8
Copyright © text Diana Bell Brooks 2013
Cover design: Nicole Edwards, Charliejack Creative Studios

First published 2013
Reprinted 2017

GINNINDERRA PRESS
PO Box 3461 Port Adelaide SA 5015
www.ginninderrapress.com.au

Contents

Part One	9
Lake Cargelligo	11
A Feat of Aerobatics	13
Memory's Pool	15
Flood Warning for Molong	17
A Formation of Poets	19
The Well	20
The Way Place	21
Running into Trouble	23
Winter in Forest Reefs	25
Dark Branches	26
Part Two	27
The Photography Lesson	29
The Birthday Eve	30
An Angel at Waterloo Station	32
Moving the Scenery	35
A Portrait of Marie Antoinette	36
La Conciergerie	38
Part Three	41
Promises	43
Four Strong Winds	44
My Uncle's House	46
Mission Bay, Auckland	48
The Chiffley Apartments	50
The Mute White Swan	51
Sketch of a Woman Writing	53

We travel the world to find the beautiful, but
we must carry it with us, or we find it not.
                              Ralph Waldo Emerson

The Magpie Rhyme

One brings sorrow
Two bring joy
Three a girl
And four a boy
Five bring want
And six bring gold
Seven bring secrets never told
Eight bring wishing
Nine bring kissing
Ten the love my own heart's missing.

                                        Anon

Part One

Lake Cargelligo

My heart's a busy sewing machine
as I lay down lines
of poetry.

Blue winter sky.
A tree throws eucalypt arms
into the street –
thirties facades
cheek to cheek with sixties modern.

They slide trays in the bakery;
voices in the hatch
ring clear.
The cooler above me's a harnessed wind,
water in its throat,
from the dwindling Lachlan river.

My neck cranes
like a tortoise
to catch sight of the town
to see life continue in its own,
winding way.

Now, the sun's off the street outside, falling
in a geometric pool,
the shape of the iron roof.

In the street,
cars cruise by
like boats
nosing things out of the way.
An aerial view of the lake
passes on the side of a truck.
The desert mirage:
all roads lead to Lake Cargelligo.

A child skips, legs into the sunshine,
and a four-wheel drive shelters
under weeping gum blossom.

A Feat of Aerobatics

I remember my father in his new baby Austin,
on the hill that tumbles down
to Balmoral Beach,
and on the ferry in the afternoon,
umbrella furled, on his way
to the newspaper office.

He'd moved us from New Zealand
in 1954, and in time
purchased for us
a more than acceptable house:
a Californian bungalow,
where my mother and I
trailed a scent of difference
before the neighbours.

Later, he gambled on a range of shares
– staking us all
on the gold futures market –
and in those early years, played golf,
throwing his club after the balls
he hit into trees.

Like the pilot in Africa trying to land
as his plane sucked in a hawk
through its plastic nose cone
– my father had miscalculated.

One-eyed he scanned the figures
of the stock exchange,
our family fortunes
heaving in the sea.
He watched the fuselage sink,
water crawl and slide like mercury
as it moved into the wings.

There was an attempt to inflate the life raft,
but it sank like a shark
with a belly pain.
Our family sat with him
immobilised in a bell of air
slung along the bottom of the sea,
our hair disintegrating.

Memory's Pool

Rotorua

There's a letter
from my grandmother, Dagmar,
to me on my fifth birthday,
telling me her parents on their wedding tour
visited the famous terraces nearby
within days of the eruption –
Mt Tarawera 1887.

And there's an old coin,
whose shine, like a dull mirror,
I'm rubbing away, to find
the image underneath
of my old country,
buried pink and white terraces,
scarred and overlaid by lava.

I think of pink jelly and coconut lamingtons
at my eighth birthday party, where I watched
in amazement in Australia
as slippery slides glazed
the air of our backyard,
and children I hardly knew
spun down, sweetened in some child-sugar
transformation.
And my parents amongst them
eager as party clowns
to fit in.

Instead I turned,
picked up the deep-tongued stones
my mother brought with us from New Zealand,
and dropped them
into the bottom of the car.
They slipped from my hands
into memory's pool
and skulked, like rainbow trout
released into new territory.

In the centre of Rotorua,
beneath the window of this hotel
figures in black cross
wet tar roads.

In the distance steam rises from fissures
in the volcano's skirts.
White ghosts of cloud
linger and wrap the land.

Flood Warning for Molong

1

In the old ticket room
at the wooden station where I write,
I pack up my papers.

Kangaroos peep shyly
from the forest shadow.
Water rises from the creek beyond
in rivulets.

Like characters captured in a tapestry
there are people from the town's long past
seeking pleasure
in the swollen creek.
They take their ankle boots off
and wade.

My father's ghost floats by the platform,
in his old white armchair.

2

When my parents travelled
by liner to Australia
they knew where they were going,
my only task to iron handkerchiefs
of thin white cotton
for the journey

Now I'm going somewhere
even more uncharted,
somewhere where the light
glances off the sea
in a curtain of coloured streamers
loved fingers holding the other end.

I can hardly part
the way of the crowd
leaning from the handrail
of the ship.

People swarm past me
in a flood that scoops me up
and draws me
into the lacquered bosom
of the lounge and stairwell
and into the centre,
where the light-roof is.
All the stairs of the ship
centre round us.

We encounter
the feel of the ark,
and the wooden railway building rises,
golden, on the breast of the flood.

A Formation of Poets

Becoming a poet is like
joining the Meteor Conversion Unit.
We spend a week together
preparing for the arrival of our comets.

We are placed
in rows in the instruction theatre,
gazing at the unmanned whiteboard.
We share shiraz from bottles,
exchange notes on oddities,
watch a girl's red hair
snake down the back of a chair.

Flying, metaphors shake us together.
We rename the unit
the Mincer Conversion Unit.

And, like a mother pecked to death by her chickens,
we are plucked clean
by criticism.

The Well

My eyes adjust to the dark
peering through bird glasses
to see the bottom.

The well's mouth lined with wood
covered over with deep rusted
chicken wire,
descends –
divided by a central ladder –
into the deep
dry soil;
parched,
tonguing
its way
into the earth.

Finally, a shard of sparkling
light…

I walk away, stop,
find a large rock. Cool.
Light drops through
the metal tank stand
and the glaring, fading sun
of the winter afternoon
blinds
like sixpence caught.

The wind keeps on. The
sun falls on my hands
as I write, warming them.

The Way Place

Roos nuzzle the evening dew.
She follows the wheel ruts,
and finds a clay pan cupped
within the earth's curve.

She's wrung
the record of those days
when Ed rode the wagon;
across limestone plains
at dusk and in the heat,
he and his father paused
at the edges of streams
to water the horses and camp.

So many years later now,
she's turning over this small scatter
of honeycombed clay.

'Is it easier to leave a granddaughter
than to leave a country?
You left me open to adventurers
who did me harm.'

The family lowered his coffin into the grave
at a mountain cemetery,
planted a tree on top of it,
and stopped her words

Endlessly she recreates him.
'We're resting our feet together
in the clay pan.'
Underfoot the clay surprises, soft and springy.
Her crinkly pale hair and dark coat stand out,
a husk against the red.

The air is cool.
The plain extends to the horizon,
as do the old creek lines.

They settle like two native birds
on the cusp.
Their voices break the silence,
as vermilion bars of sunset
crumble, like embers in a grate.

Running into Trouble

Just as her legs begin to fail her,
she runs into Trouble
on the sand dunes
and falls face-forward,
ninepin down.
She's been running
hatless, trying to reach town.

He is handsome, patient, well-suited,
waiting for her in his car
and offers her a lift –
but he goes the wrong way.

The car slides along the sand
beside the sea,
carrying her off
to a cultivated house.
As they go, she sees Frank walking
to an empty seat on the esplanade.

The light flashes off the sea
as she arrives.
People in dark clothes
move wheelchairs out of the sun,
switch the television on.

Back in her tiny room,
dressed more revealingly,
Trouble shows up again
holding a mirror
to her sleeping face.

There she is, the heroine,
with the brown curls of a younger self,
now framed by the dark rim of his hood.
'Tell me, who are you?'
she tries to say.

But no mist forms
on the mirror.

Winter in Forest Reefs

Bad winters
are long and single minded
nerve-racking and finger cracking.
With limitless horizons of hills
they circulate winds in overcoats
strike out luck and light,
recycle garbage under snow.

The winter in Forest Reefs,
disturbed his bantam,
hung it by a foot in the wire fence.

When he came home from Bloomfield,
finding bloodied feathers on the path,
he wanted to go back to Lake Cargelligo,
where light glanced off the lake.

Then spring bore down the gully
striking as he opened the cottage door
tearing at the line and plunging on.
A parrot in the great pine above him
bared its red throat and spun in the wind.

On trips to town to visit his priest,
he saw stands of wild white pear blossom
bloom at the dark foot
of the old volcano, Mt Canoblas.

Winter as ever, played the joker;
in his photographs, his fibro cottage
assumed a mantle of snowy beauty.

Dark Branches

I outrun the afternoon birds
and escape down
bush pathways.

Through dark branches,
I watch the sea,
hang up the dew
in frangipani flowers.

The path home
gets steeper.
My mother lies
on a green couch,
suspended in sleep,
still, draped
in a transparent wrap
slipping from her shoulder.

I see she's been sewing motifs
from my old dresses,
the carpet an appliqué
of frayed shapes.

Watching through
a living tree:
an opera house moon.
A silver needle
threads me
into sky.

Part Two

The Photography Lesson

Midwinter in the Orange Botanical Gardens.
We're snapping purple flowers close up;
not ladies' bonnets now but silk tassels,
hanging sweet and loose.

This spring we fly to Europe.
The photographer rehearses
our travel shots,
still more, our future selves,
in front of the tiny church building,
above the heritage roses.

Down on the arched church path
we add to ourselves
a depth of perspective,
but look back and see
through the silver millennium arch
a remnant of our party,
still unclear on the other side.

The photographer and I
walk beside the billabong.
The lesson all but over,
I call up memories of music
from the hill beyond

The bluestone stage
keeps the future under wraps.

The Birthday Eve

On the eve of Elisabeth's birthday
we slip into our swimsuits,
and like feminine figures by Matisse
show each other
our pale brown selves

and with what long fingers
we plait napkins
for the celebration later –
like children,
at play in our thatched doll houses
echoing Breton ritual.

We move outside a cottage
and receive guests,
drink Bombay Sapphire Gin.
Our hair leans down
in willow fronds, fresh
with unexpected autumn growth.

Shadows displace
white gravel chips at our feet
and join hems with the European fir trees.

As we go inside,
the TV news announces
Mary Jane Simpson
has disappeared in Rio.

Becky,
– ever the mystery writer –
files notes
as she makes room for us.

I linger by the window,
the last to join the circle,
recall my own stolen childhood,
mystery never to be solved.

How our lives
surprisingly interweave,and blend,
as we join liana-like in eager talk
around the oaken table.

An Angel at Waterloo Station

for Howard Jacobson

Bent over her drawing
she bites into a *Pain au Chocolat*.
Her wings droop slightly,
dragging a little towards the dust
like an oak bent to the lawn.
Then, looking up, she flushes
and I see how young she is.

The famous four-faced clock
is suspended above us
under interleaving glass.

I turn back to my engagement
with *The Guardian*, and my coffee.
There I find word of you
after thirty years.
Tomorrow you are discussing your latest novel
at Finchley North Library at 10 a.m. –
just as I will be carried smoothly out
on the Eurostar to Paris.

So many years since we talked of Dickens
meeting by appointment in the Sydney rain.
You the Englishman
and I the student –
our friendship
a series of moments,
never quite connecting
even as we loitered later
on Waterloo Bridge
reluctant to abandon
a shared past.

I confirm my ticket
on the international concourse,
and unpick my way
down a flight of limestone steps,
threading my suitcase
through the crowd
into a world of pickpockets,
and down-at-heel Africans.

Yet this too has the air
of no-man's-land,
where shotguns sound.

Like university corridors,
where you escaped
with a bust of D.H. Lawrence
under one arm
and flew back to London.

I hear a scuffle just behind me
and sneak a glance back:
a tall bald-headed man
is swooping at people's heels
for cigarette butts.

I feel like a heroine
in a black and white Dickens illustration.
Without warning, a kind of melancholy
grace, opens a way for me
into the world
of modern England.

Today, I've come into my inheritance.

A black taxi pulls away.
A train whines and scrapes overhead
coming in, cracking and bending,
past the Wellington Hotel.

Moving the Scenery

i.m. Martin Johnston

Paris was awake
and moving the scenery
of her dawning streets
when she thought she saw Martin
in a café on a hill in Montmartre.

A Greek-Australian poet,
Martin made literary salons
of every room he stepped into;
talking of the Sea Cucumber
or Blood Aquarium.

When he opened his typewriter
and began a conversation
with himself
a café became a community.

But the mistress in the wings
of Writer's Heaven
could not revive this poet.
She watched him hide his hands in sleeves,
then lay them, like dead fish,
on the table.

Out of the café mirror
was that Martin staring back?
He vanished as she looked.

A Portrait of Marie Antoinette

Among the pictures of the Revolution
I look longingly down
to the refreshing shade of the park.

But again my eyes turn back.
There is my husband Louis, the king
saying goodbye to his family,
to us, in our nightwear
my son the Dauphin and I.
Soldiers wait, tightly leashed
at the doors.

Then at the guillotine,
my exasperating husband,
still patiently arguing the point
on the short stepped road to his execution.

All day the limitless parade
of worldly public passes;
at night the evening wind
blows through our upper floor
prising out the empty corners.

I've lived my life in rooms
muffled by curtains of voile,
have patiently embroidered
scenes of idyll.
Now I exist behind picture glass.

Yet still I count the threads I sew,
think only of tiny Louis, Dauphin,
ripped from me
with the rising of every sun
dressed in toy robes
for his portraiture.

La Conciergerie

Pushed from behind,
my foot seeks out the stairs,
finally finding comfort
in the grooved tiles
of the cell on upper floor.

They have made mementos
of my life
in these last months;
images of me
austerely clothed
with my rosary beads.

My gaolers are still playing cards;
I need to rest for a moment
in the same room,
behind a flimsy screen.

God, who visits me here,
wraps me in tiny drops of shade,
maple leaves, shapes of sky.

They will take me downstairs soon
before the tumbrels arrive.

For me, I long for the lifting of my hair
for cutting; the throwing of my curls
on the plain wood counter;
the ripping of my collar,
ready for the blade.

Death is His embrace.
He will relieve me
of the weight
of my rings, my crosses and my hair.

They will serve for others –
as signposts to the unknown.

Part Three

Promises

A ghazal

A blizzard of English magnolias came in late winter
and a company of robins, promises

of fertility and blossom, open hands of gifts towards me
as if to say I warranted your promises.

Instead you left me, moving in slow motion
and slipping on street ice, pondering your promises.

Broken china rained from my mouth,
the bitter taste of tea spoke of your promises.

Yet my blame breaks two ways I suppose,
how threadbare the link that bound us – mere promises.

But now in verse I bring you sheeted home,
still believing in your promises.

Four Strong Winds

Simon's fingers were long and thin
with dark hairs.
He strummed
the song he was practising –
Four strong winds
that blow lonely…

Steady and kind –
he lifted me over two years of study
of European kings and queens
in the sunset-emblazoned Fisher Library;
but he never starred,
not even in his own drama.

One night –
his mother and sister away –
I ironed his jeans
in their lounge room.
Around us a café of steam
and his sister's empty wheelchair
mocked us from the corner;
Simon, watching me,
was unaccountably upset
because I didn't iron
jeans with creases.

The fact of his sister's lolling limbs
hung over the fibro house
and, in time, his sister's presence
even extended
to the palm fronds near the library.

The glow of sunset beams
reached the booths, touching
hair and the wood of tables.
Beside the two us at study,
Simon's mother would carefully
put his sister to bed,
in a golden blanket.

My Uncle's House

The net fender leans against the fireplace,
your elbow on the smeared arm protector.

We've sat together these past few years,
sharing secrets,
family and military,
mending the fabric of our two lives
over wine and conversation.

The windows of the house steam up
with the breath
of absent guests.

The lamp is a pendulous African flower
shadowing the wall.

In my childhood your postcards
from Malta, Italy, Russia and Britain
turned my eyes towards the world.

And I remember sitting at my school desk,
studying history,
wondering if this would be the day
one of the world's commanders
would push the red button.

But now as I wait for news of you
bad weather falls;
water drops from ivy.
Gracing your music stand,
a model of the Vulcan bomber
you flew for the Royal English Air Force.
The wine box I sent last Christmas
still sealed and on the floor.

There's a smear of blood on the couch blanket,
a head-sized hole in the wooden wall
on the stairway landing.
Here you fell, opening up
a silent cry in the house.

You were making your way
on half an engine,
your tenacious grip on the controls,
mirage of village lights before you,
your head in a cockpit of dark

Mission Bay, Auckland

1

My mind mulls
on the human shape and scale of things
of letting things be,

to nestle like shells
securely in the hand,

from moment to moment
like the small hand
clasped in mine.

2

We build a sandcastle
in Mission Bay:
pippies, limpets and tower shells

A rampart with windows
overlooks a moat,
watches the brimming tide.

Triangles of sail slice
pale zircon waves,
a sand carpet unravels

rectangles of light
to the toes of Mt Rangitoto;
a lizard sleeping in the afternoon.

3

My brother and I once flew
on his bicycle down to the sea,
I clung to him proudly
sheltered by his arms,

and paddled in the nursling waves.
The sea covers his ashes now
and speaks of him.

4

Waves curl and slip, clouds edge
this small clear world
constructed out of memories.

My granddaughter is four,
and I, half a century more,
another sea, another country away.

But I watch the sea slip back
and know, only this sea
speaks the truth to me.

The Chiffley Apartments

The Bach concerto
is a nimble flute of sound,
a will-o'-the-wisp.

Nerves of waiting are tensed,
her arms the bones of a kite, ready
to fling itself into the air.

She hears his footfall in the room.
The music slows, changes
dropping her into the pleasure of it,

and finishes;
a silence of lilacs.
in the half-lit apartment.

With the bar counter,
sleek armchairs
and glassed-in view,

cars slide along the roads below,
and windshields wink on the bridge.

The Mute White Swan

1

By Eden park,
sails glove the wind,
and yachts buffet the glass sea.

I summon the zircon green
of Auckland Harbour
for me to rest in endlessly,

raise a sea goblet to my lips
with a bouquet of stone and ash,
of white seashells.

In the soft Auckland grass
I find a mute white swan
in unfamiliar territory.

The swan contains her joy
and heaps her nest
with foxglove stems and petal sheets,

and in Albert Park at night,
she hangs up incandescent
images of herself.

2

The *pohutukawa's* arms measure for us
the steepness of the hills,
after the tsunami.

Together we descend.
Trees wear their roots
as beards diving down the air.

The wharf eases with the sea flow.
My swan and I take supplies
to a golden vessel strung with lines of poems.

My soul's hunger is met.

Sketch of a Woman Writing

She holds her shoulders stiffly,
like a bent tree,
her arm winged
as she writes,
yet a soft lichen
scarfs her neck.
Her hand curves into the page,
sparkling with a lake blue ring.

The book she leans on
is her notebook of sketches,
feeding
the roots of her thoughts.

Her body make
the Tree of Life:
objects fruit there.
Her scarlet glasses case
opens an inner eye,
visionary, unblinking,
held in a frame of wood.

www.ingramcontent.com/pod-product-compliance
Lightning Source LLC
Chambersburg PA
CBHW062204100526
44589CB00014B/1952